The Norwegian Buhund

A Complete and Comprehensive Owners Guide to: Buying, Owning, Health, Grooming, Training, Obedience, Understanding and Caring for Your Norwegian Buhund

Dog Care Professionals

Copyright © 2016 Dog Care Professionals

All rights reserved.

Although the author and publisher have made every effort to ensure that the information presented in this book was correct at the present time, the author and publisher do not assume and hereby disclaim any liability to any party for any loss, damage, or disruption caused by errors or omissions, whether such errors or omissions result from negligence, accident, or any other cause.

ISBN-13: **978-1543056327**

The Norwegian Buhund

CONTENTS

Introduction 10

Description 11

    Lifespan 12

    Height and Weight 13

Breed Characteristics 14

Why Should You Purchase A Dog? 15

    Companionship 15

    Exercise 16

    Watchdog 16

    Nurturing 16

    Empathy 17

Dog Equipment Basics and Essentials 18

    Collars and ID Tags 18

    Leashes and Harnesses 19

    Bedding 20

    Food and Water Bowls 22

Worms, Ticks and Fleas 23

Toys 24

Expanding your Collection 26

Basic Cost of Owning a Dog 27

Initial costs 27

Basic Equipment 27

Preventative Health Care 28

Food 29

Grooming 29

Training, Dog Care and Walking 30

Purchasing Your New Pet 31

Breeders 31

Pet Stores 32

Rescue 32

Puppy Care 34

Find a Good Vet 34

Food 35

- Feeding Schedule 35
- Obedience Training 36
- Bathroom Training 37
- Be Social 38
- Signs of Illness 38
- Spaying and Neutering 39

Dog Care 40
- Dog Food 40
- How much to Feed Your Norwegian Buhund 41
- Visits to the Vet 41
- Exercise 42

Grooming 44
- Grooming Tools 44
- Grooming a Short Haired Dog 45
- Bathing your Dog 46
- Brushing your Dogs Teeth 47
- Ear Cleaning 48

- Nail Clipping 49

Training 51

- The Key Components of Training 51
- Pre-requisites for successful training 51
- Preparation 52
- Clicker Training 52
- Teaching Focus and Attention 53
- General Training Tips 54
- Avoid Punishment 55
- What if the training is not working? 55

Illnessess 57

- Hip Dysplasia 57
- Parasites 58
- Cherry Eye 60
- Incontinence 60
- Parvovirus 61
- Dental Problems 62

Ear Problems 63

Dangerous Foods 65

Avocado 65

Grapes and Raisins 65

Chocolate 66

Coffee and Caffeine 66

Macadamia Nuts 67

Xylitol 67

Yeast 67

Onions, Garlic and Chives 68

Peaches, Pears and Plums 68

Cooked Bones 69

Alcohol 69

Other Substances to Avoid 70

Extra Things to Consider 71

Vacation 71

Pack Animals 71

Begging 72

Introducing a New Baby to your Dog 72

Location 73

Final Thoughts 75

ABOUT THE AUTHOR 76

Other Popular Books by Dog Care Professionals ... 77

INTRODUCTION

Before purchasing any pet it is important to understand that as a pet owner you are responsible for the care and wellbeing of your pet. It is important to try and learn as much as you can about the animal you are considering to keep as a pet to make sure that your lifestyle, household and financial status are suited to provide your pet with the best possible care. This guide has been designed to provide you with both precise and concise information about a Norwegian Buhund's basic needs to help you provide your pet with the best quality care practices. This guide will give an in-depth explanation on training your Norwegian Buhund, raising your Norwegian Buhund from a puppy, grooming, health care and everything in between!

DESCRIPTION

The Norwegian Buhund is a breed of dog that is a member of the Spitz typing. The Norwegian Buhund is also commonly known as the 'Norsk Buhund' and the 'Norwegian Sheepdog.' The breed is closely related to the Icelandic Sheepdog. In the excavation of the ancient Gokstad, a Viking grave from about the year 900 A.D, in Norway multiple skeletons of dogs that closely resemble the Norwegian Buhund were discovered which suggests that the Norwegian Buhund is an ancient breed of dog. The Norwegian Buhund has traditionally been used for the purpose of herding sheep and other cattle. However it has also been commonly used as a watch dog, a nanny dog and as a companion dog. The breed is medium-sized and has a square profile that has a high set tail that curls over the center of its back. The Norwegian Buhund's coat comes in either a black or wheaten coloration: which is any shade from pale cream to a bright orange. The temperament of dogs is normally affected by the following factors: individual personality, heredity, training and socialization. It is therefore important to make sure that you meet the puppy's mother before purchasing a Norwegian Buhund. It is also important to make sure to thoroughly socialize your Norwegian Buhund with strangers, children and other animals during its puppyhood. Generally speaking, the

Norwegian Buhund is known to be an active, cheerful and loyal breed. The Norwegian Buhund makes a great addition to any family home due to their affectionate nature and love of children. However it is important to always supervise a Norwegian Buhund while it is interacting with children due to the breed's high levels of energy and hyperactivity – while the Norwegian Buhund is not known to be an aggressive breed it is not uncommon for a Norwegian Buhund to become overly excited and knock small children over in playful excitement. The Norwegian Buhund forms extremely close bonds with its family unit and may be aloof with strangers. The Norwegian Buhund is also an incredibly head strong and intelligent breed that desires to learn new things on a regular basis. It is important to note that as a working breed, the Norwegian Buhund has a high amount of energy which needs to be expended. If the Norwegian Buhund has a buildup of energy it is likely to develop destructive behaviors due to boredom or hyperactivity. It is also important to note that the Norwegian Buhund does not tire easily and it is therefore a full time pursuit to keep your Norwegian Buhund well exercised.

Lifespan

A Norwegian Buhund will normally live to be between 12 and 13 years old. However it is not uncommon for a Norwegian Buhund to live to be as old as 15, providing that it does not develop any serious health issues.

Height and Weight

A fully grown Norwegian Buhund will normally stand between 16 to 18 inches (40.6 to 45.7cm) tall at the shoulder. A healthy adult Norwegian Buhund will normally weigh between 25 to 40 pounds (11.3 to 18.1kg). It is important to note that the weight of a healthy Norwegian Buhund depends on how large the Norwegian Buhund is – taller Norwegian Buhund should weigh more.

BREED CHARACTERISTICS

The following section will give you a simplistic overview of the characteristics of a Norwegian Buhund. Our rating system is from 1 to 10 – with 1 being the lowest score and 10 being the highest.

- **Adaptability:** 6/10
- **Friendliness:** 8/10
- **Health:** 8/10
- **Ease of Grooming:** 5/10
- **Amount of Shedding:** 6/10
- **Trainability:** 6/10
- **Intelligence:** 7/10
- **Exercise Needed:** 10/10
- **Playfulness:** 10/10
- **Family Friendliness:** 10/10

WHY SHOULD YOU PURCHASE A DOG?

In the United States of America it is estimated that there are between 70 and 80 million pet dogs owned and over 40% of the county's households own a dog! As the statistic shows dogs are incredibly popular pets – but why? Any dog owner will happily tell you all the benefits and joys of owning a dog! The following section will outline 5 key benefits of owning a dog:

Companionship

Dogs are incredibly loyal and loving animals and make a great addition to any household. If you build a strong relationship with your pet they can transcend just being a pet and become a friend, or ever a member of your family! However your dog brings you companionship in other ways. You are more likely to interact with strangers while walking your dog than if you were walking alone. Owning a dog also allows you to go to dog parks and converse with other dog owners. If you walk your dog around your neighborhood on a regular basis, you may also develop a friendly relationship with your neighbors who own dogs as you are likely to pass each other several times a day.

Exercise

Owning a dog increases your chance of exercising due to the fact that you will need to play with and walk your dog. Taking your pet for frequent walks will decrease your chance of becoming over weight. A recent study in Australia found that children with a pet dog are 50% less likely to be overweight! Exercising on a regular basis has a plethora of other health benefits such as reducing the chance of heart disease, strokes and high blood pressure. A dog can be a great exercise companion as well as being a great motivation due to the fact that it is cruel to not provide your dog with adequate exercise.

Watchdog

Dogs are very territorial, loyal and aware as a species. Even from as early as puppyhood, a dog is able to detect potential burglars and dangers. Your dog will bark at anything suspicious or out of the ordinary which will alert you to any potential trouble. Most criminals are instantly put off by the barking of a watchdog.

Nurturing

The majority of humans have a deep desire to nurture. This desire used to be fulfilled by caring for, and raising, a baby or caring for younger siblings. Across the Western World the average family size is decreasing which makes pets the perfect outlet for people's nurturing desires. In families with no children, or one child, dogs are fulfilling the role of being substitute children and siblings! Dogs are intelligent beings and respond well to being nurtured which makes it a positive and rewarding experiences for both the owner and the pet. Dogs also seem to nurture children. Children who own a dog tend to have a high self-esteem and are more popular with their classmates!

Empathy

Dogs are incredibly empathetic animals! They will sense the mood of their owner and either attempt to provide comfort, through physical contact, or a distraction through a humorous playful act. It is not uncommon for dogs to bring their distressed owners their favorite toy as an attempt to cheer them up. Dogs have also saved their owners from countless dangers – such as house fires and burglaries.

DOG EQUIPMENT BASICS AND ESSENTIALS

Before purchasing a Norwegian Buhund it is important to make sure that you have already purchased all the equipment you will need to provide your new Norwegian Buhund with the best possible care. Ensuring you have all the essential equipment before purchasing your pet is the best way to build a strong relationship with your pet and to keep it content, happy and healthy.

Collars and ID Tags

Purchasing a collar with an ID tag is arguably one of the most important things you can purchase for your Norwegian Buhund. The collar allows you to attach a leash to your Norwegian Buhund, which in turns allows you to take your pet for a walk which is essential to their health. There are a wide range of collars available to purchase made from multiple different materials and styles. It is important to take your dog's habits into account when purchasing a collar. For example if your dog regularly enjoys swimming it is not advisable to purchase a leather collar. It is also important to not purchase a thin collar! When you walk your Norwegian Buhund on a leash it may lunge, or pull, which will cause the collar to dig into its neck. The wider the collar is the wider the area the force from the lunge is spread over – basically wider collars are more comfortable! The ID tag allows for your pet to be easily identifiable and returned to you if they are ever lost! We recommend having your Norwegian Buhund's name and your home address on the ID tag. This will allow the person who finds your dog to keep it calm by using its familiar name and will know where to return your pet to.

Leashes and Harnesses

Purchasing a lead, or harness, is vital in ensuring your Norwegian Buhund remains healthy! Having a lead, or harness, allows for you to walk your pet and provide them with the exercise they need. Walking your pet also helps to create a strong bond and friendship between the two of you. There are a few differences between Leashes and Harnesses which will be explained below:

> ➢ **Leash:** Most dog owners will use a leash while walking their pet. Leashes ensure both comfort and safety when you take your dog out for a walk. It is important to buy a leash that extends to allow your dog to explore and move away from you at times. It is equally important to buy a sturdy leash that will allow you to keep control of your pet for

the entirety of the walk.
- ➢ **Harness:** If you have a large, small, energetic or boisterous dog a harness may be a safer option. The harness is safer for these types of dogs as they will not feel discomfort from their collar when they pull against the leash. Purchasing a front-clip harness (that goes over the dog's chest) will allow you to have more control over your pet.

Bedding

Some owners allow their dogs to sleep in their beds or on their sofas. While this can definitely be a great way to build a strong relationship with your dog it is also important to purchase a suitable bed for your pet. By providing your pet with its own bed it will give your dog a place of its own to feel safe and secure. There is an overwhelmingly wide variety of dog beds available in pet stores and on the internet. We recommend adhering to the following criteria when purchasing a dog bed to ensure both practicality, safety, comfort and warmth.

- ➢ **Natural Materials:** It is important to make sure the dog bed you purchase is made of natural materials. Synthetic products, including fire retardant and stain-proof chemicals, may be harmful to your dog's

health.
- ➢ **Removable Cover:** If you purchase a dog bed that has a removable cover it allows for you to regularly and easily clean your dog's bed. Keeping your pet's bedding clean is essential to keeping your pet healthy as it removes bacteria and any parasites that may have found their way into the bedding. Purchasing a bed with a removable cover also allows you to replace the cover if it keeps overly worn and ripped – replacing just the cover is a lot less expensive than replacing an entire bed!
- ➢ **Non-Skid Bottom:** When your dog dives into its bed you do not want it to slide across the floor as this could cause damage to your pet, the bed and the floor. Purchasing a bed with a non-skid bottom removes the chance of injury and damages.
- ➢ **Plan Ahead:** If you are buying a puppy it is important to remember that your puppy will grow! It is considered best practice to purchase a bed that is the correct size for an adult dog so it will not be out grown.

There are two main categories of beds that are suitable for dogs. It is important to watch your dog sleep so you have an idea of how its sleeping preferences and how it physically lies down. Choosing the correct bedding is vital to ensure your dog feels safe and secure at home. The two categories of bedding are as follows:

- **Round / Nest-Style Beds:** These beds are ideal for smaller dogs and larger dogs who like to curl up when they sleep.
- **Raised / Cushion / Futon Beds:** These beds are ideal for dogs who enjoy stretching themselves out when they sleep.

Food and Water Bowls

It is important to purchase a food bowl and a water bowl for your pet Norwegian Buhund. There are three main materials that are used to create these bowls: plastic, ceramic, stainless steel. The following section will outline the pros and cons of each material.

- **Plastic:** Plastic bowls are cheap, durable and long lasting. The only downside of a plastic bowl is that plastic can be toxic to dogs if ingested. If you notice your dog gnawing at its bowl you should replace it with either a ceramic or stainless steel bowl.
- **Ceramic:** Ceramic bowls are very stable and heavy which makes them a good choice if your dog pushes its bowl while it eats or

drinks. The main downside of using a ceramic bowl is that they are porous and will therefore need to be thoroughly cleaned on a daily basis.

➢ **Stainless Steel:** Stainless Steel bowls are recommended by vets and dog care experts. They are easy to clean, easy to sanitize, durable and inexpensive. Similar to when purchasing a dog bed, it is considered best practice to purchase a stainless steel bowl with a non-skid bottom to prevent the bowl from moving while your dog eats or drinks.

Worms, Ticks and Fleas

Part of your responsibility as a Norwegian Buhund owner is to control and kill the parasites that your Norwegian Buhund will definitely get at some point. Worms, Ticks and Fleas can cause serious discomfort and health issues if left unchecked. There are medicated collars and shampoos that help to minimize your Norwegian Buhund's chance of getting fleas and ticks. There are also medicines you can purchase to help prevent both external and internal parasites. It is considered best practice to take your pet to your local vet and ask for them to give you a prescription for medicines to control parasites.

Toys

Toys for your Norwegian Buhund are essential for so many different reasons! Toys can provide your pet with mental and physical stimulation which can also lead them to having less destructive behavior patterns – such as chewing up furniture! Chew toys can also have dental health benefits. Toys also allow you to build a strong and fun relationship with your pet. The following list details some of the most popular toys available on the market:

> ➢ **Chew Toys:** Chew toys can provide your dog with hours of solo fun and can also help your dog to develop a strong and healthy jaw. Before giving your dog a chew toy it is important to check that it is not too hard – an overly hard chew toy can have the opposite effect and damage your dog's jaw! A good rule of thumb is to bang the chew toy on your knee – if it hurts it is too hard for your dog's mouth! It is likewise important to make sure that your dog does not ingest any of the chew toy though as the plastic, or rubber, is toxic!
> ➢ **Tug Toys:** Tug toys are a very popular choice as they allow for you to actively play with your dog. It is important to not allow your dog to become aggressive while you play

with the tug toy! To avoid your dog becoming aggressive you should keep a positive and happy inflexion in your voice. The most popular choices for tug toys are ropes and squishy plastic bones.

- **Balls and Fetch Toys:** Balls and fetch toys are another great way to actively play with your pet. It is important to purchase fetch toys made of soft plastic so your dog will suffer no dental damage or physical pain (if they miss the catch and get hit by the toy). A good choice for fetch toys are ball, Frisbees, cuddly toys and squishy plastic sticks. Tennis balls are a common choice for fetch but are not actually a healthy choice of toy! The covering on Tennis balls can actually abrade the enamel on your dog's teeth which can lead to serious health, and dental, issues in later life.
- **Food-Dispensing Toys:** Food-dispensing toys are a great way to mentally stimulate your dog. They come in a variety of different styles and shapes. We recommended purchasing a ball or cube as it will also allow your dog to push the toy around which encourages physical activity as well.

Expanding your Collection

Dogs are incredibly intelligent beings and, like humans, have preferences when it comes to bedding, food and how they have fun. Once you have developed a good understanding of your new Norwegian Buhund's preferences we recommended taking these preferences into account when purchasing new equipment and food.

BASIC COST OF OWNING A DOG

Owning a dog obviously costs money – but how much money? The following section will provide you with the average cost of owning a dog to help you decide whether you are in the correct financial state and to help you budget for any unexpected bills! It is important to remember that on average, dogs live for between 8 and 18 years.

Initial costs

- **Purchase of Dog:** Most Norwegian Buhund breeds cost between $200 and $1500.
- **Microchip:** If your Norwegian Buhund has not been microchipped before purchase this will cost $50.
- **Lifetime Council Registration:** This costs $49 for desexed Norwegian Buhund and $182 for Norwegian Buhund who have not been desexed.

Basic Equipment

- **Dog Bed:** Dog beds normally cost between $20 and $200.
- **Brush:** Most brushes designed for grooming

cost around $20.
- ➢ **Food and Water bowls:** Each bowl costs are $20 and you will need a minimum of two – one for water and one for food.
- ➢ **Collar, Lead, Tags and Harnesses:** A complete set will normally cost between $50 and $200.
- ➢ **Toys:** Dogs need a range of toys. We recommend setting aside between $50 and $100 dollars to provide your dog with the enough toys.

Preventative Health Care

- ➢ **Vaccination:** Vaccinations cost between $50 and $120 depending on which ones you get. Your dog will need vaccine at 8, 12 and 16 weeks of age and then every 3 years after that.
- ➢ **Worm Tablets:** Tapeworm and Heartworm prevention tablets cost about $10 a month.
- ➢ **Fleas:** Most flea prevention cost around $10 a month.
- ➢ **Bi-annual Vet Check:** You will need to take your dog for a health check at the vet every 6 months. A general health checkup costs around $65.

Food

- **Basic Food Needs:** Basic food (kibble) will cost you around $1,200 a year.
- **Treats:** Treats are not essential but most owners enjoy giving them to their dogs. We recommend budgeting around $100 a year for dog treats.
- **Dental Chew Sticks:** Dental chew sticks are a great way to improve your dog's jaw strength and dental hygiene. We recommend budgeting around $100 a year for dental chew sticks.

Grooming

- **Shampoo and Conditioner:** Shampoo and conditioner will normally cost around $30 a year. It is not necessary to buy expensive brands of shampoo and condition – basic products designed for dogs will work perfectly fine.
- **Visit to the Groomer:** Groomers normally charge between $50 and $150. We recommend taking your dog to the groomers at least twice a year.

Training, Dog Care and Walking

- **Puppy Training:** Puppy training normally costs around $100 for a month long training course.
- **Advanced Training:** Most owners enjoy taking their dogs to obedience classes and advanced training. These services normally cost around $170 for a month long course.
- **Dog Walking:** Dog walking normally costs around $25 an hour (depending on where you live).
- **Daycare:** Daycare services normally cost around $50 a day.
- **Boarding:** We recommend budgeting around $300 a year on boarding services. Most boarding services will charge around $50 a day.

PURCHASING YOUR NEW PET

There are multiple different ways to purchase a dog: from a breeder, from a pet store or from a rescue service. There are pros and cons of each method and they will be explained in the following section.

Breeders

When it comes to purchasing a Norwegian Buhund, breeders are unarguably the best method. A breeder will allow you to interact with your Norwegian Buhund before you purchase it. This will allow you to understand the Norwegian Buhund temperament and behavior as well as allowing you to inspect the Norwegian Buhund for any genetic defects. Breeders are normally a part of a registered service – such as The Kennel Club. By being a member of a registered organization it gives the breeder accountability and legitimacy. Breeders will be able to inform you of any issues with the Norwegian Buhund and how they have been socializing it. Breeders will also be able to tell you the exact birthdate of your new Norwegian Buhund. The only downside of breeders is the fact that they are more expensive than pet stores – however this should not be an issue when you are considering purchasing a Norwegian Buhund.

Pet Stores

Pet stores are a common choice when purchasing a new Norwegian Buhund – but we HIGHLY do not recommend purchasing a Norwegian Buhund from a pet store! Most pet stores purchase their Norwegian Buhund from puppy mills. Puppy mills are notorious for breeding and raising their Norwegian Buhund in terrible conditions which leads to both behavioral and health problems. Employees at the pet store will most likely not be able to provide you with specific information about a Norwegian Buhund – they are unlikely to know its exact date of birth and health background. The pedigree of a Norwegian Buhund from a pet store is also questionable. Pet stores have a terrible return policy! It is not uncommon for a new owner to not have fully considered every aspect of owning a Norwegian Buhund and they therefore return it. If you return a Norwegian Buhund to a breeder you can be assured that the Norwegian Buhund will lead a happy life. However, if you return a Norwegian Buhund to a pet store it will most likely be euthanized, if it has grown to be older than a puppy, due to the fact that it is unlikely to sell.

Rescue

If you are an experienced Norwegian Buhund owner you may considered getting a Norwegian Buhund from a rescue shelter. Most Norwegian Buhund from rescue shelters are free and the shelter just wishes you to make a donation. It is important to remember that rescue Norwegian Buhund may have health or behavioral issues due to their turbulent lives. Norwegian Buhund in rescue shelters are also hardly ever puppies and tend to be middle aged or older. However by getting your Norwegian Buhund from a rescue shelter allows you to give a Norwegian Buhund a better life than they would have had in the past. Most Norwegian Buhund that end up in shelters have been cruelly treated or abandoned and by adopting one you are giving the animal a chance to experience life in a loving home.

PUPPY CARE

When purchasing a Norwegian Buhund both first time owners and veteran owners normally opt for buying a puppy. Purchasing a puppy will allow you to establish a good and healthy relationship with your dog and will set the foundation for a long happy friendship. Another reason puppies are so popular is due to the fact that they are among some of the most adorable creatures on the planet! However caring for a new puppy is not the easiest thing. You will have to be prepared to make some huge lifestyles changes to accommodate your new puppy. The following section is a simple and concise guide to help you care for the new canine addition to your family.

Find a Good Vet

Before purchasing your puppy it is a good idea to research the vets in your local area. It is very important to find a vet that is local and highly qualified. The best way to find a good vet is by asking your friends, local dog walkers, local dog groomers, asking the breeder and researching online. Once you purchase your new puppy you should take it straight to your vet for a checkup. The checkup visit will make sure that your puppy is in good health and free from any serious birth defects or genetic health issues. Introducing your vet to your new Norwegian Buhund while it is young also allows for your puppy to become familiar with the vet – this can help avoid stress during later visits. By taking your puppy to the vet straight away, it also allows you to start a health care routine with your pet. It is important to set up a vaccination plan with your vet and also to discuss the best methods for control parasites (both internal and external).

Food

It is important to purchase food that is formulated specifically for puppies. A decent brand will have a statement from the Association of American Feed Control Officials (AAFCO), or your countries equivalent, on the packaging to ensure that the food you are purchasing is going to fulfil your puppy's nutritional requirements. Small and medium-sized breeds can start eating adult dog food when they are between 9 and 12 months of age. Larger breeds of dog should be fed on puppy kibbles until they reach 2 years of age. It is important to make sure that your puppy has cool, fresh and clean water available to them at all times.

Feeding Schedule

Puppies have a different feeding schedule to adult

dogs. Their feeding schedule changes as they get older. We recommend feeding your puppy on the following schedule:

- **6 – 12 weeks old:** 4 meals per day
- **3 – 6 months old:** 3 meals per day
- **6 – 12 months old:** 2 meals per day

Obedience Training

It is important to train your new puppy to be obedient. Obedience will allow your puppy to have a life full of positive interactions as well as forging a stronger bond between you and your pet. It is important to teach your puppy simple commands such as sit, stay, down and come. These commands will help to keep your dog safe and under control in any potentially dangerous situations. We recommend attending a local obedience training class. Obedience classes allow for you and your dog to learn the best methods for each process and command. Obedience classes also allow you, and your puppy, to interact with other people and dogs of all ages and from all backgrounds. It is important to remember that positive reinforcement has been proven to be a dramatically more effective process than punishment.

Bathroom Training

Housetraining is a priority if you want to keep your house clean! Before you start your housetraining it is important to locate a suitable location for your puppy to go to the bathroom. If your puppy has not had all of its vaccinations it is important to find a bathroom that is inaccessible to other animals. This will help to avoid your puppy getting any unnecessary viruses or diseases. There are three key tricks to keep in mind when you are attempting to housetrain your puppy: positive reinforcement, planning and patience. It is important positively praise your puppy when they go to the bathroom outside and not to punish them when inevitable accidents will happen. We recommend the following times to try and introduce your puppy to a bathroom routine:

- When you first wake up.
- When your puppy wakes up from any naps it might have.
- During and after physical exercise.
- After your puppy eats or drinks a lot of water.
- Immediately before bed time.

Be Social

The main way to avoid your puppy developing behavioral problems is to be social with it. At approximately 2 to 4 months old, most puppies will begin to accept other animals, people, places and experiences. It is important to start socializing your puppy with as many people and animals as possible. We recommend bringing your puppy to a dog park, to your friends or relatives houses, to dog friendly restaurants and to have other people accompany you while you walk your pet. By interacting with multiple different types of people and animals your puppy will learn to be more social and accepting.

Signs of Illness

It is important to watch your puppy closely to make sure that it is not exhibiting any signs of illness. Your puppy is at its most vulnerable stage of its development while also being at its most important stage of development. If you notice any of the following signs you should take your puppy to the vet immediately: lack of appetite, vomiting, lack of weight gain, lack of growth, diarrhea, pale gums, nasal discharge, inability to pass urine and stool, lethargy, swelling and difficulty breathing.

Spaying and Neutering

There are a lot of factors to considered when deciding if you should spay or neuter your puppy. Many owners refuse to spay or neuter their puppy due to the fact that they find it morally wrong and unnatural. However most owners do decide to have their pet neutered. Shelter euthanasia is the number one killer of dogs and companion animals throughout America. In Atlanta alone over 15 million dollars is spent annually on euthanizing unwanted dogs! The only way to avoid this is to have your pet spayed or neutered. Dogs face some discomfort if they are in heat or are unable to mate. Spaying and neutering creates no long term health problems for your pet. At the end of the day it is an important decision for you and your family to make. We advise talking it over with your vet and family/friends who have already been through the process.

DOG CARE

Once your puppy has grown up, or if you have purchased an adult Norwegian Buhund, you will need to change how you care for it.

Dog Food

There are so many different brands of dog food available: organic, all natural, hypo-allergenic, vegetarian and even vegan! Good dog food is vital to provide your pet with the nutrition it needs to reach its full potential both physically and mentally. Good nutrition helps your Norwegian Buhund fight disease, prevents obesity, minimizes your dog's chance of getting an illness and generally improves your Norwegian Buhund's overall health and happiness. It is important to remember that the advertising on dog food is aimed at humans – because we are the ones that pay for it! You should only feed your dog food that has been approved by the Association of American Feed Control (AAFCO) as it will ensure that the food is both safe and nutritious. You should look for brands of dog food that claim to have an 'AAFCO approved complete and balanced nutritional value' – it is illegal for a brand to claim that they have been approved by the AAFCO if they have not. Make sure the food you purchase contains protein, carbohydrates, fats, vitamins and minerals.

How much to Feed Your Norwegian Buhund

Unfortunately there is no exact method for figuring out exactly how much an individual Norwegian Buhund should eat. Determining the correct size meal depends on the type of dog food, how many times a day your dog eats, your dog's size and weight, your dog's metabolic rate, the amount of exercise they get and many other possible variants. Adult Norwegian Buhund are normally fed twice a day. We recommend looking at the feeding guide on the packaging of your dog's food. The feeding guide is normally recommends weights of food based upon your dog's weight. However this feeding guide is not necessarily accurate (your dog may struggle gaining weight or may gain weight at an increased rate). We recommend talking to your vet about how much you should be feeding your Norwegian Buhund. It also takes a bit of time to get used to your Norwegian Buhund and their eating habits.

Visits to the Vet

It is important to take your Norwegian Buhund to the vet on a regular basis. Regular visits to the vet can allow you to treat any issues your Norwegian Buhund has in the early stages to avoid them having a negative impact on your Norwegian Buhund's health. We recommend scheduling to see your vet at least twice a year – however more frequent visits are advantageous in identifying health problems! It is more important to prevent the onset of disease rather than treat them once they occur. With each visit to the vet you should make sure that you get your dog weighed. By getting your dog weighed on a regular basis you will know if you are feeding it the correct sized portions.

Exercise

Exercise is vitally important to keep your Norwegian Buhund happy, healthy and behaving correctly. Dogs, and puppies, have a lot of energy and may develop destructive behaviors if they are not allowed to burn off their energy. How much exercise a dog needs is dependent on its age, breed and health. Most Norwegian Buhund should be walked for at least 30 minutes a day – however we recommend walking your Norwegian Buhund for around 60 minutes a day to ensure it has gotten enough exercise. You will know when your Norwegian Buhund has had enough exercise when it has slowed its walking speed by a considerable amount. Good exercise uses both physical and mental muscles. We therefore recommend providing your Norwegian Buhund with multiple different sources of exercise such as: hiking, walking around your block (using different routines), taking your Norwegian Buhund to the park and taking your Norwegian Buhund swimming. If you provide your Norwegian Buhund with a lack of exercise they are likely to become obese. Obesity in Norwegian Buhund, like in humans, comes with a wide range of health issues. Obesity contributes to a dog developing diabetes, respiratory disease, heart disease and general ill health and tiredness. We recommend living by the following philosophy: a tired dog is a happy, healthy and good dog.

GROOMING

Grooming is an important aspect to caring for your Norwegian Buhund! Grooming includes caring for your Norwegian Buhund's coat, dental health, nails and over all cleanliness. Dogs enjoy getting messy so sometimes cleaning can be a chore! The following section will highlight all the aspects of grooming that you should consider.

Grooming Tools

- **Bristle Brush:** Bristle brushes are used for all breeds of dog. Bristle brushes help to keep your dog's coat shiny and free from dirt.
- **Clippers and Shedding Blade:** Most species of dog will need to have their coats trimmed in summer to keep them cool. We recommend using clippers for dogs with long coats and shedding blades for short hair dogs.
- **De-Matting Rake:** De-matting rakes have long wire prongs. These prongs are great for removing matts from long coats. It is important to use this tool gently to avoid causing your dog discomfort.
- **Rubber Brush:** Rubber brushes are great for

removing dead hair. They create a massaging effect which many dogs enjoy.
- **Slicker Brush:** Slicker brushes are used to remove tangles and dead hair. They have rows of bent wire pins. They should only be used on dogs with long or thick hair.
- **Nail Clippers:** Nail clippers should be scissor shaped to allow for best control. It is important to purchase sharp nail clippers and to always have a spare set (in case one set become blunt).
- **Nail File:** Nail files are used to file the end of your dog's toe nail after it has been clipped. It is important to purchase a high quality nail file as it will allow the filing process to be completed much quicker.

Grooming a Short Haired Dog

Short haired Norwegian Buhund should be brushed a minimum of once a week. Brushing your Norwegian Buhund's coat will stimulate natural oils in their skin and will also remove any dead hair. You should groom your short haired Norwegian Buhund by brushing all over its body with a slicker brush. Make sure to start at the head and work your way down. It is important to keep your Norwegian Buhund's coat taut as you brush to effectively remove dead hair. Once you have removed all of the Norwegian Buhund's dead hair you should brush the Norwegian Buhund's coat back into the position it naturally lies in. We recommend using a bristle brush or a rubber brush for this process. You can also comb your dog's coat. A short haired dog will not have excessive tangles in its coat and a fine toothed brush is a perfect way to make your dog's coat look perfect!

Bathing your Dog

Just like people, dogs need a good bathing schedule. Most Norwegian Buhund only require a bath once a month. However if your dog enjoys rolling around in mud and getting especially dirty, you may have to bathe it more often. It is not recommended to bathe your Norwegian Buhund more than once a week as it will lose the essential oils present on its skin. It is important to use a Norwegian Buhund friendly shampoo and conditioner when bathing your Norwegian Buhund as they are designed to not irritate your Norwegian Buhund's skin. If your dog has especially sensitive skin it is possible to purchase medicated shampoo to decrease the chance of irritating your dog. We recommend washing your dog in either your bath tub or shower, as it is the least likely to create a watery mess! It is considered best practice to provide your pet with a non-slip mat to keep them secure in the shower or bath tub.

Before bathing your dog make sure to have your shampoo and a towel ready to hand. While bathing your pet you should keep one hand on your Norwegian Buhund at all times to make sure it does not leave the bath / shower. If your Norwegian Buhund is worried about the bathing process reward them with treats to encourage them to relax. You should aim to massage your Norwegian Buhund during the shampooing and toweling process to make the bathing experience more pleasurable and fun for them.

Brushing your Dogs Teeth

In America it is estimated that 80% of dogs have some form of dental disease by 3 years of age! Norwegian Buhund, like humans, need to have their teeth cleaned to remove bacteria and tartar build up. If you do not clean your Norwegian Buhund's teeth they are likely to develop Periodontal disease which affects the base of the tooth near the gum line. Norwegian Buhund can also suffer from dental disease such as gingivitis. It is recommend using a meat flavored toothpaste to reward your Norwegian Buhund when it lets you brush its teeth – these toothpastes have the added benefit of being nontoxic if swallowed! You can use a regular toothbrush or a finger brush for the cleaning process. Make sure that the brush has soft bristle to avoid damaging your Norwegian Buhund's teeth and gums. Aim to brush each individual tooth for around 5 seconds. It is considered best practice to brush your Norwegian Buhund's teeth on a daily basis. Daily cleaning is the best way to prevent dental problems and to keep your Norwegian Buhund's breath smelling dramatically better!

Ear Cleaning

Dogs have very long ear canals (around 5 to 10cm in length) that have a right angled bend in them. The bend means that foreign objects can easily get into your Norwegian Buhund's ear canal but are very hard to get out! If your Norwegian Buhund gets water in its ear, the water can pool at the bend and cause ear infections due to the warm, moist and dark environment of the ear. You should ask your vet how often you should clean your Norwegian Buhund's ears, but as a rule of thumb: no more than once a week and no less than once a month. To clean your Norwegian Buhund's ears you will need ear cleaner, cotton wool and treats to reward your dog during the potentially uncomfortable process. There are multiple different brands of ear cleaner available and it is important to choose a good quality product. We recommend asking you vet for their suggestion as most pet stores will stock different brands. Once you have the products to hand it is time to start the cleaning process. Gently hold the flap of your dog's ear upright and fill the ear canal with the ear cleaner. It is important to aim the ear cleaner directly downwards as you use it. Once the ear cleaner is in place, massage the skin around your dog's ear to mix the ear cleaner with the contents of your Norwegian Buhund's ear canal. Do this for around 20 seconds. Once the massaging time is up, stand up and move away from your dog. Your dog will shake its head vigorously to remove some of the ear cleaner. Once your dog has stopped shaking its head, grab the cotton wool and use it to wipe the folds at the opening of your Norwegian Buhund's ear canal until it looks clean. Make sure to reward your Norwegian Buhund before and after the ear cleaning process to relax it.

Nail Clipping

It is important to trim your Norwegian Buhund's toe nails every two weeks to keep them properly maintained. If you allow your pet's toe nails to grow too long it will cause your Norwegian Buhund discomfort as it walks – the long term consequence of walking on overly long toe nails is arthritis! It is important to use clippers that resemble scissors as they provide the most control while clipping your Norwegian Buhund's nails. It is also considered best practice to use small clippers as they again allow for better control. Make sure that your clippers are sharp before attempting to clip your pet's nails. Gently separate your Norwegian Buhund's fingers for clipping – never squeeze your Norwegian Buhund's toe as they will cause them to be in pain. It is considered best practice to have an assistant during the clipping process as they are able to secure your dog in place and distract it's attention. You should aim to make the clipping process and a positive experience so your dog feels at ease – use positive praise and treats to promote a positive atmosphere! It is IMPORTANT to note that all Norwegian Buhund have a vein that run through their fingers called a 'quick.' If you cut off too much of your dog's nail it is possible to cut into the 'quick' which will cause your Norwegian Buhund to bleed. Although not fatal it is still to be avoided as it will cause your pet unnecessary discomfort. If you do accidentally cut the 'quick' you should stop the bleeding by dabbing a little cornstarch onto the nail with a cotton swab. It is also possible to file your Norwegian Buhund's nail or have a vet cut your pet's nails for you (although this will have a fee). If you are worried about trimming your dog's nails we recommend taking your Norwegian Buhund to a vet once to have them demonstrate how to trim your pet's nails correctly.

TRAINING

It would seem that Norwegian Buhund enjoy being trained due to the fact that they both enjoy the human interaction of the training process and seem to enjoy 'pleasing' their owners. Training your Norwegian Buhund is a perfect way to strengthen the bond between you and your pet as well as being a cool thing to show to non-dog owners.

The Key Components of Training

The following bullet points are the five most important aspects of training any animal:

- Trust
- Positive reinforcement
- Repetition
- Patience
- Consistency

Pre-requisites for successful training

It is vital that your Norwegian Buhund are well socialized and accustomed to both your presence and being handled by you. It is not a good idea to try to train new Norwegian Buhund immediately after purchasing them as they will not trust you and may be frightened or stressed by the training process. Younger Norwegian Buhund, and puppies, are generally more adaptable to training and will therefore pick up new tricks at a faster rate. However younger Norwegian Buhund will also have a shorter attention span which can make the process of training them a long process. Older Norwegian Buhund will have a longer attention span but may be less willing to do physical based training.

Preparation

Before starting to train your Norwegian Buhund it is best to know how your Norwegian Buhund enjoys spending it's time and what food it loves so you can reward it appropriately. It is important to find one or two healthy treats to reward your Norwegian Buhund with to help them stay healthy and motivated during the training process. We recommend rewarding your Norwegian Buhund with the following treats: raw carrot, a liver treat or a small piece of chicken. The reason it is important to know your pet Norwegian Buhund's preferences is to allow you to work with your pet's natural inclinations and to praise and positively re-enforce the behavior you want.

Clicker Training

Clicker training is considered the easiest and most

effective way to train Norwegian Buhund. The concept behind the training is that the clicker tells your Norwegian Buhund when they have correctly performed a trick or action. Using a click also allows you to signal to your dog that they have done something correct from a long distance away. Clickers allow you to shape your dog's behavior, which means praising and rewarding closer and closer approximations to the behavior or trick you wish to teach. A click should always be paired with a treat. This allows your dog to create an association between 'clicks' and treats which will encourage your dog to obey clicks. You can purchase a specialized dog training clicker from any pet store or online. Before using the clicker in training, you should pair a click with a reward. Simply click then give your dog a treat. Then wait a few seconds and repeat the process. Repeat this around 10 to 15 times so your dog knows to associate clicks with treats before the training session has even begun.

Teaching Focus and Attention

The fundamental aspect of training a Norwegian Buhund is to teach the Norwegian Buhund to pay attention to you. You should say the dog's name and then reward them for their attention once they give it to you. Repeat this process several times to ensure that your dog will respond with the appropriate level of attention when you call its name. It is important to shape your Norwegian Buhund's behavior through positive reinforcement until you can get your dog to give you full focus – including eye contact.

General Training Tips

The most important training tip is to make sure that you always keep training session short. Short training session will reduce the chance of your dog becoming frustrated and will likewise enhance its concentration. We recommend keeping all training session between 10 and 15 minutes in length. Remember to always reward your Norwegian Buhund after clicking to reinforce the likelihood that they will obey clicks. If you are teaching a tricky command, we recommend giving your dog a 'jackpot' of treats when they do the desired trick. By giving your dog more treats than normal will signify that they have done the correct action. It is considered best practice to never end on a failure! If your Norwegian Buhund has not fully come to terms with a new trick, you should end the training session by rewarding your pet for completing a trick they already know. This will keep your Norwegian Buhund looking forward to training sessions.

Avoid Punishment

Dogs do not learn well by being punished. Punishment will normally make your Norwegian Buhund feel confused, stressed and scared – which are not good mental states to be in for learning! A dog that destroys a piece of furniture and looks guilty is responding to your anger rather than knowing what they did was wrong. If your dog is doing something destructive we recommend clapping your hands loudly, or calling its name, to get its attention. Once you have its attention you should lead its focus onto a more productive activity.

What if the training is not working?

It is important that you go into the training process with the intention of having fun and bonding with your pet – any tricks your pet learns will be an added bonus! It is very uncommon for a Norwegian Buhund to be untrainable. If the training is not working it is important to think about if you have a close relationship with the Norwegian Buhund you are trying to train and if your Norwegian Buhund is in the correct mind set to learn tricks. Norwegian Buhund can easily become bored of repeated training and may likewise be disinterested due to the time of day. Another reason for a dog's disinterest may be that you are offering them the wrong type of treat as a reward. It is important to remember that dogs, like humans, learn at different rates and some Norwegian Buhund will therefore take longer to train. If a Norwegian Buhund seems impossible to train it is probably advisable to stop trying to train it and just enjoy playing with it and caring for it.

ILLNESSESS

There are multiple factors that play a huge part on your Norwegian Buhund's health: your dog's genetics, the quality of veterinary care they receive, what they eat and how safe the environment they live in is. The following section aims to help you recognize the most common and major threats to your dog's health to allow you to treat and prevent them. Your Norwegian Buhund's health is vitally important to giving your Norwegian Buhund a chance at a long, happy and healthy life.

Hip Dysplasia

Hip dysplasia is a heritable condition that prevents the thighbone from fitting snugly into the hip joint. Hip dysplasia is common among Norwegian Buhund but does not affect them all. It normally has symptoms of pain and lameness. However, hip dysplasia does not always cause your Norwegian Buhund discomfort but it may develop into arthritis as your Norwegian Buhund ages. Hip dysplasia is incurable and Norwegian Buhund who have it should not be bred. When purchasing a puppy from a breeder you should ask for proof that neither of your puppy's parents have hip dysplasia.

Parasites

Dogs enjoy spending a lot of time outside where they lick and sniff everything, roll around in dirt and puddles and run through long grass. While they find these activities enjoyable they also lead to parasite infestations.

- **Fleas and Ticks:** Fleas and ticks are the most common parasites. Fleas breed incredibly quickly and a couple can turn into an infestation surprisingly quickly. Ticks can cause some very dangerous disease – such as Lyme Disease and Ehrlichoisis. You dog will repeatedly itch itself, either with its paw or against furniture, if it has a tick or flea infestation.
- **Skin Mites:** Skin mites are dramatically smaller than fleas and ticks. Skin mites live on, or burrow into, your Norwegian Buhund's skin and can cause sever discomfort and diseases such as Mange. The main symptoms of skin mites are itching, skin irritation, inflammation and hair loss.
- **Heartworms:** Heartworms are parasites that migrate through your Norwegian Buhund's internal system to their hearts and other major organs. Due to the locations they

infest, they are extremely dangerous and usually deadly! The most effective way to prevent heartworms is to use a monthly heartworm preventive – medication that can purchased from your vet. There are no symptoms for heartworms other than your Norwegian Buhund becoming very ill.

➢ **Intestinal Worms:** Intestinal worms are very common among puppies. If your dog has recently had a tick or fleas there is a good chance that they now have an intestinal tapeworm. If your Norwegian Buhund eats other Norwegian Buhund's feces there is also a high chance that they will have an intestinal worm of some sort. The most common way to know if your Norwegian Buhund has worms is to physically see the worms in your Norwegian Buhund's waste. The best method to keep your Norwegian Buhund worm-free is to have a vet perform a fecal test at least once a year.

➢ **Single Cell Parasites:** Single cell parasites live in your dog's digestive tract. They can cause both Giardia and Coccidiosis if left untreated. If you are giving your dog heartworm preventative medication you normally do not need to worry about single cell parasites as the medication should kill them as well.

Cherry Eye

Cherry eye is a problem that more commonly affects certain breeds but can affect any dog. The main symptom of cherry eye is a large red swelling appearing at the inner corner of one your dog's eye. Cherry eye is caused by the prolapsing of a tear gland attached to your dog's third eyelid. The prolapsed gland swells forward and creates the red bulge. Cherry eye is not a vision threating illness but does cause your Norwegian Buhund a lot of discomfort. There are a lot of websites and guides for curing cherry eye at home but we recommend taking your Norwegian Buhund to the vet so it receives the best quality medical care from a trained professional. There are two surgical options, performed under general anesthetic, to treat cherry eye. The first is to remove the damaged tear gland completely. The second it to surgically manipulate the gland back into its correct position. We advise that you consult with your vet as to what the best course of action is for your Norwegian Buhund's specific case.

Incontinence

Incontinence can affect your Norwegian Buhund at any age. If your Norwegian Buhund has previously been housetrained, it is important to remember that a loss of bladder, or bowel, control is a physical problem not a behavioral one. Incontinence is most commonly found in older Norwegian Buhund, especially females. Incontinence is normally caused by the following reasons: a urinary tract infection, old age, stress and anxiety, neurological problems (such as seizures), recent spaying surgery, diseases and other health problems. If your dog is suffering from incontinence it is recommend to bring it straight to the vet. The vet will be able to diagnose what is causing the problems and will be able to provide a suitable solution.

Parvovirus

Canine parvovirus is the both highly contagious and most deadly viral disease that affects dogs and puppies. Puppies have an increased chance of catching this illness. Most un-vaccinated dogs who catch parvovirus will die. However, parvovirus is not a fatal illness is identified in its early stages. The best method to prevent parvovirus is to give your puppy, and Norwegian Buhund, a full course of medical shots to provide it with strong protection and immunity from the virus. It is also vital to keep your puppy away from other Norwegian Buhund and animals before they have been fully vaccinated! The symptoms for parvovirus are: vomiting, lethargy, a fever and diarrhea. These symptoms are very common for a lot of other less serious illnesses but you should still take your pet to the vet if you notice any as you do not want to risk your dog having untreated parvovirus.

Dental Problems

Most dental problems in dogs are cause by periodontal disease. Periodontal disease can affect more than just your Norwegian Buhund's mouth and gums! If your Norwegian Buhund has rotten teeth and highly damaged gums they are more likely to catch other illnesses. More dental hygiene can cause your Norwegian Buhund to commonly get inflammations throughout their body. The best way to provide your dog with top quality dental care is to provide it with a chew toy. Chew toys allow your dog to strengthen their teeth and jaw as well as removing tartar! There are also multiple different types of doggy dental treats available which are designed to clean your dog's teeth and freshen their breath – Win Win! It is also considered best practice to clean your Norwegian Buhund's teeth, either by taking your pet to a professional dental cleaning service, a veterinary clinic or by brush your Norwegian Buhund's teeth yourself using a toothbrush. You should strive to make dental care a core part of your dog's grooming routine. The key signs for a dental disease are: excessive drooling, loss of appetite, difficulty eating, broken teeth, loose teeth, inflamed gums, tartar buildup and very pale gums. If you notice any of the above symptoms we recommend taking your dog to the vets.

Ear Problems

The majority of ear problems are relatively easy to treat once they are diagnosed. Ear problems can either be chronic (reoccurring) or acute (one off). Ear infections are one of the most common type of ear problem found in Norwegian Buhund. Ear infections normally occur in the external ear canal and have symptoms of ear redness, scabs and discharge around your dog's ear canal. This type of ear infection is called 'Otitis' and is caused by either a bacterial infection, a yeast or fungal infection, allergies or over exposure to water (such as swimming and bathing). The second most common type of ear problem is an infestation of ear mites. If your dog has ear mites there will be symptoms of black discharge around the ear canal, redness and inflammation of the ear canal, scabbing and a very strong odor. It is best practice to take your dog to the vet if they have any of the above symptoms as the vet will be able to identify the cause of the problem and be able to provide your dog with the best type of medical care. It is considered best practice to not clean your dog's ears before taking them to the vet – your vet will need to see the symptoms of your dog's ear problem. Most ear problems can be corrected through a treatment of oral medication or ear drops.

DANGEROUS FOODS

When owning any pet it is important to know what you should and should not be feeding it. Dogs are no exception to this! There are multiple different foods that can cause sever health problems in Norwegian Buhund – some can even be fatal! Foods that are commonly eaten by humans (both healthy foods and indulgent foods) can be incredibly toxic to Norwegian Buhund. It is important to educate your family and guests on what a Norwegian Buhund can and can't eat to avoid someone feeding it something that could damage its health. The following section will outline foods that you should NEVER give to your dog:

Avocado

Avocado leaves, pits, bark and fruit contain a toxin called 'Persin.' While Persin is harmless to humans it has been known to cause breathing difficulties, stomach problems and fluid retention and buildup in the chest. An Avocado's pit is also incredibly dangerous as it will obstruct your Norwegian Buhund's gastrointestinal tract if swallowed.

Grapes and Raisins

Both grapes and raisins have been known to cause

seriously health problems in Norwegian Buhund – such as liver damage and kidney failure! It is not currently known what specific chemical in grapes and raisins is toxic to Norwegian Buhund. It takes as little as a handful of grapes to seriously poison your dog!

Chocolate

While chocolate is viewed as a treat for humans, it is definitely not for dogs. Chocolate contains a chemical called theobromine which is toxic to Norwegian Buhund. Theobromine will cause a dog to vomit and have diarrhea. It also has the potential to cause seizures and long term damage to your pets nervous system and heart! It is important to watch children around your dog as they may, with the best intentions, feed your Norwegian Buhund some of their chocolate.

Coffee and Caffeine

Both coffee and caffeinated products can be fatal if ingested in a high enough quantity. Coffee and caffeine have similar negative effects to chocolate. It causes vomiting, abnormal heart palpitations, seizures and long term damage to the dog's nervous system. It is important to remember that caffeine can be found in a high number of products such as: energy drinks, tea, chocolate, cocoa beans and medicine.

Macadamia Nuts

It can take as little as five macadamia nuts to have a seriously negative effect on your dog's health. The symptoms of macadamia nut poisoning include muscle tremors, vomiting, rapid breathing, rapid heartrate, increase body temperature and signs of general weakness. If macadamia nuts are mixed with chocolate the combination of poisoning will nearly always be fatal.

Xylitol

Xylitol is a sugar based alcohol that can commonly be found in gum, candy, sweet baked goods and other sugar-substitute items. Xylitol causes no apparent harm to humans but is extremely toxic to dogs. Even a small dose of Xylitol can cause seizures, low blood sugar levels, liver failure and even death in Norwegian Buhund!

Yeast

Yeast can be found in basically any dough products (bread, cakes, etc). Yeast will rise and expand in your Norwegian Buhund's stomach in a similar manner to how it rises in bread. A small amount of yeast will cause your dog mild discomfort and to be gassy. However if your dog ingests too much yeast it is likely rupture their stomach lining and intestines! It is important to never feed your dog bread or any other products containing yeast.

Onions, Garlic and Chives

It does not matter what form these produces are in (powdered, raw, cooker, dehydrated or mixed with other foods) they are always detrimental to your Norwegian Buhund's health. Onions, garlic and chives contain sulfoxides and disulfides which can cause anemia and damage to your Norwegian Buhund's red blood cells. Onions, garlic and chives also cause vomiting, breathlessness and general weakness in Norwegian Buhund.

Peaches, Pears and Plums

Peaches contain pits that are potentially a choking hazard to dogs. The pits also contain amygdalin which contains a compound made up of cyanide and sugar that degrades into hydrogen cyanide when metabolized. Hydrogen cyanide is incredibly toxic to dogs and will normally lead to death! Pear seeds contain a small amount of arsenic which is likewise dangerous. Plum pits cannot be digested properly and will therefore cause intestinal obstruction which can cause multiple dangerous health issues. It is important to check your backyard for any trees that produce large fruits and seeds. If you find multiple seeds in your dog's waste it is probably best to cut down and remove the tree.

Cooked Bones

There is a common misconception that all bones are good for Norwegian Buhund. While chewing uncooked bones can help improve the strength of your Norwegian Buhund's jaw and provide them with need nutrients, cooked bones are highly dangerous. Cooked bones can easily splinter into sharp, and jagged, pieces. These sharp splinters can tear the lining of your dog's throat or stomach. They will also cause your dog a lot of discomfort as they pass the splintered pieces of bone.

Alcohol

Alcohol has the same effect on a dog's liver and brain as it has on a humans. However the effects of alcohol are greatly amplified on dogs and it therefore takes a lot less alcohol to cause damages – the smaller the dog the greater the effects. A small amount of alcohol can cause vomiting, diarrhea, depression, difficulty breathing, comas and death! Alcohol can obviously be found in beer, liquor and wine but can also been found in some food.

Other Substances to Avoid

The following substances are considered less harmful but should still not be given to your Norwegian Buhund: chewing gum, baby food, apple seeds, corn on the cob, fat trimmings, salmon, tuna, milk and dairy, tobacco, salt, raw meat and raw eggs.

EXTRA THINGS TO CONSIDER

The following sections are extra things to consider that did not fit into any of the above sections.

Vacation

It is likely that you will have a vacation at some point during your Norwegian Buhund's life. It is important to remember that not all vacations will accommodate your pet Norwegian Buhund. It is therefore best practice to try and line up at least 3 people who would be willing to care for your pet Norwegian Buhund while you are away, before even purchasing a Norwegian Buhund. Some pet care stores provide a care service for owners while they are on holiday so it is also advisable to ask your local pet store if they offer this service. Another alternative is kennels and boarding services.

Pack Animals

Dogs are pack animals and enjoy being social with humans, other animals and other Norwegian Buhund. If you are going to be away from home for long periods of time (for example at work) it is considered best practice to purchase more than one Norwegian Buhund. It is important that your Norwegian Buhund does not feel lonely as this will lead to depression and unnecessary stress.

Begging

If your Norwegian Buhund begs for food at the table, you are not alone! Begging can seem cute at first but can quickly become an annoying habit. If begging goes unchecked it can escalate into whining during meal times, jumping up onto the table and ever stealing food off plates. The best way to avoid begging is to NEVER allow anyone to feed your Norwegian Buhund from the table in the first place. However if you have already fed your dog from the table we recommend ignoring your dog's begging. Once your pet realizes that begging is a futile process they will quickly stop it. Rewarding your dog when it is away from the table, during mealtimes, is the best way to encourage it to stop begging.

Introducing a New Baby to your Dog

Dogs can become jealous. Jealousy can happen in any breed. All breeds, from Rottweilers to Pugs, have been known to bite or attack babies out of pure jealousy. The best way to make sure that your Norwegian Buhund does not become jealous is to keep to your established care routine. Do not forget to feed, walk, bathe, train and play with your Norwegian

Buhund! The first way to introduce your new baby to your Norwegian Buhund is to introduce its scent. Bring your Norwegian Buhund an item that has your baby's scent on it (such as an item of clothing) and allow your dog to become familiar with the scent. You need to make it clear that your dog needs your permission to sniff the item – this will create clear boundaries and create respect for the baby. Before introducing your Norwegian Buhund to the baby it is considered best practice to take your Norwegian Buhund for a long walk to drain it of any excess energy. It is important to make sure that the baby, the Norwegian Buhund and yourself remain calm during the introduction. Introduce your Norwegian Buhund at a distance and over time (weeks) allow it to come closer and closer to the baby. By introducing the baby slowly you are allowing your Norwegian Buhund to know that it is worthy of its respect. Most dogs have no issues with new babies! However if you are not 100% confident with the safety of your baby we recommend rehoming your dog. The safety of your baby and dog are the greatest priority (dogs that attack a baby are normally euthanized)!

Location

It is important to consider where you will be living with your new dog. If you are going to be living in a small apartment, or a house without a garden, it may be a good idea to consider purchasing a smaller breed of dog. Likewise, it is important to consider if you neighbors will be bothered by the sound of your dog barking. It may be worthwhile purchasing a breed that is known to be more silent! As a dog owner you will have to ensure that you and your dog have a suitable place to live.

FINAL THOUGHTS

Thank you for purchasing our pet care manual on caring for a Norwegian Buhund. We hope you have found the information both interesting and informative. We hope that this book has allowed you to make an informed choice on whether owning a Norwegian Buhund suits you and if so we hope that the information will help you to provide the best quality care for your pet Norwegian Buhund.

We will be publishing multiple other dog care manuals on our author page on Kindle. If you have an interest in learning more about specific dog breeds then we highly suggest you check out our other work.

Here at Dog Care Professionals we are passionate about providing the best quality information to our customers. We would highly appreciate any feedback, or reviews, you could leave us on our Kindle page to allow us to help create the best possible pet care products available on the market.

ABOUT THE AUTHOR

Here at Dog Care Professionals we are passionate about dog care. As a brand we have a strong idea of what makes up a good pet care book. We consult with multiple experts in multiple different fields to allow us to create a book filled with cumulative opinions and best practices. The experts we consult range from veterinarians to every day pet keepers who have had years of experience caring for the specific breed each book is on. Our aim, and mission, is to produce the best possible dog care books that are a great value for money.

OTHER POPULAR BOOKS BY DOG CARE

PROFESSIONALS

The
Finnish Spitz

A Complete and Comprehensive Owners Guide to:
Buying, Owning, Health, Grooming, Training,
Obedience, Understanding and Caring for Your
Finnish Spitz

Printed in Poland
by Amazon Fulfillment
Poland Sp. z o.o., Wrocław